MEINE ERSTEN TAUSEND WÖRTER

in Englisch

Heather Amery
Illustrationen von Stephen Cartwright

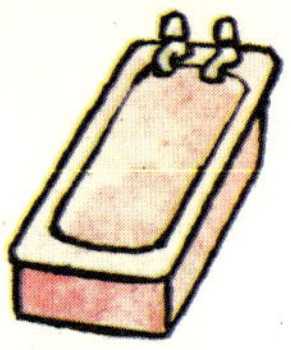
bath

soap

tap

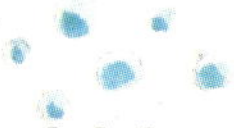
bubbles

toothbrush

water

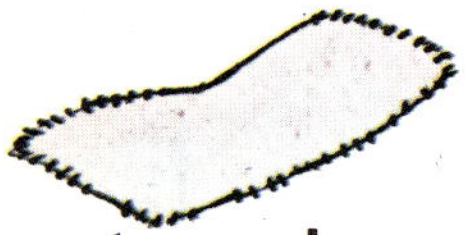
towel

sponge

shower

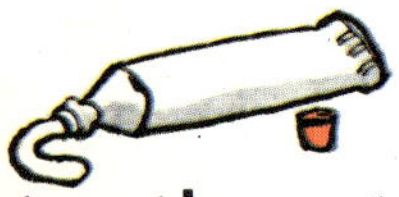
toothpaste

washbasin

toilet

bookcase

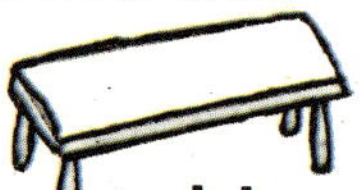
table

radio

At home

radiator

wool

wallpaper

clock

carpet

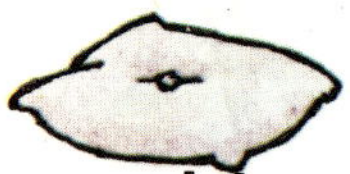
cushion

record playe

bedroom
lamp
bed
chest
brush
pillow
wardrobe
rug
pictures
eiderdown
clothes
comb
mirror
sheet
stairs
spider
hall
air
letters
telephone
cobweb
fly
newspaper
pegs

The kitchen

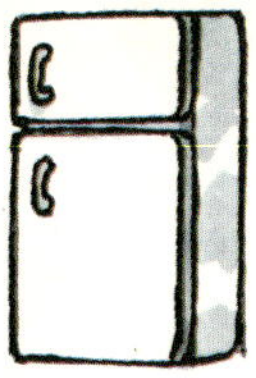
refrigerator

glasses

clock

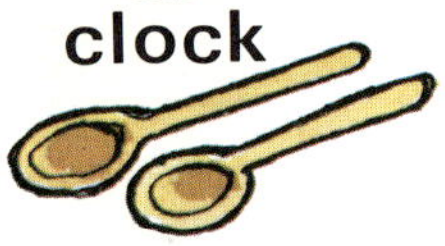
spoons

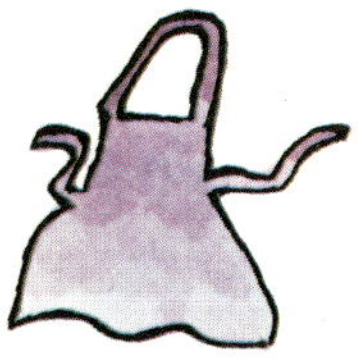
apron

switch

saucepans

saucers

iron

kettle

mop

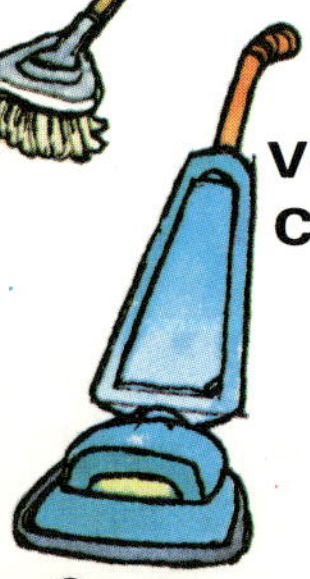
vacuum cleaner

sink

forks

door

duster

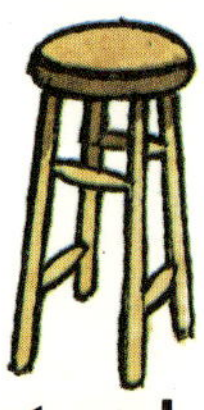
stool

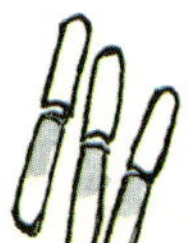
knives

polis

cooker
tiles
drawer
rubbish
frying pan
washing machine
dustpan
plates
ironing board
washing powder
brush
table
bulb
cups
teaspoons
matches
key
broom
bowls
cupboard

The garden

wheelbarrow
beehive
snail
bricks
dustbin
caterpillar
spade
ant
pigeon
gutter
ladder
seeds
shed
worm
flowers
sprinkler
bone
hedge
trowel

lawn mower

path

tree

fork

leaves

broom

hosepipe

hoe

smoke

bee

rake

pram

wasp

plants

grass

bonfire

bird's nest

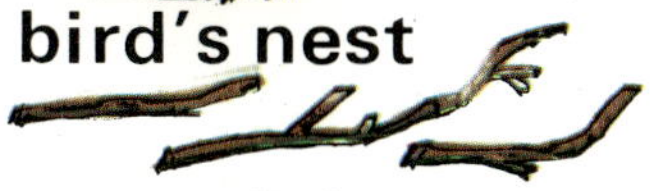
sticks

greenhouse

The workshop

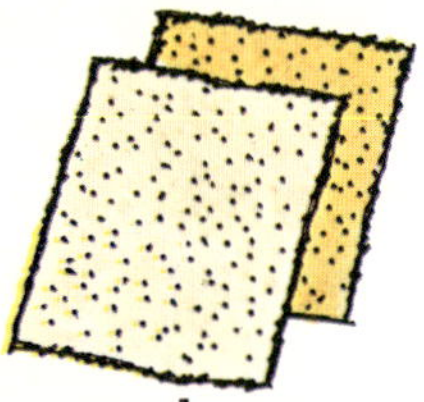

sandpaper

drill

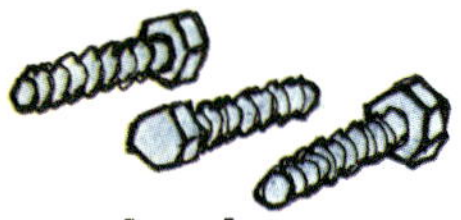

bolts

tacks

saw

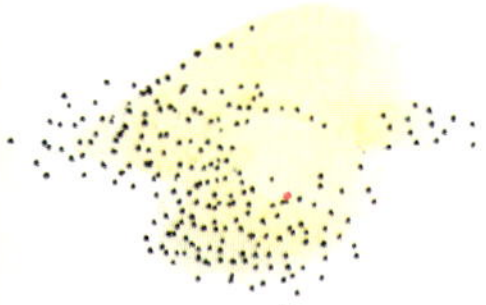

sawdust

hammer

file

tool box

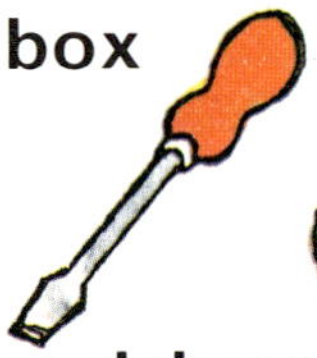

screwdriver

plank

paint pot

shavings

penknif

barrel
axe
nuts
tape measure
screws
ladder
nails
vice
firewood
bench
jars
wood
plane

garage

ambulance

bicycle

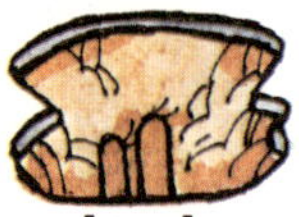
hole

café

pavement

shop

traffic lights

chimney

lorry

crossing

steps

man

The street

hotel

police car

roller

drill

school

playground

flats

statue
bus
taxi
trailer
pipes
roof
market
factory
aerial
van
policeman
fire engine
house
woman
lamp post
driver
motor cycle
car
cinema
church
igger

The toyshop

piano
cards
dolls' house
recorder
robot
mouth organ
marbles
cannon
camera
beads
whistle
rocket
dice
dolls
spacemen
rocking horse
crane
roller
blocks
bats
guitar
tool s

fishing rod
paints
clay
parachute
typewriter
boat
target
tank
soldiers
castle
money box
rain set
drums
balls
puppets
racing car
masks
trumpet
bow and arrow
gun
submarine

ball

string

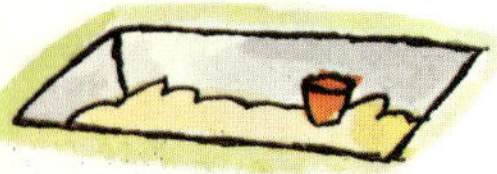
sandpit

picnic

kite

ice cream

dog

swings

gate

path

tadpoles

slide

The park

frog

bush

roller skates

children

scooter

swans
baby
earth
railings
push chair
birds
seesaw
flowers
puddle
ducklings
skipping rope
yacht
flower bed
bench
lake
dog lead
duck
trees

The zoo

panda
bat
hippopotamus
penguin
paws
kangaroo
wing
eagle
feathers
ostrich
giraffe
wolf
monkey
pelican
gorilla
bear
beaver
lion
cubs
crocodile

horns
deer
camel
seal
polar bear
apes
elephant
trunk
zebra
buffalo
tail
shark
rhinoceros
goat
dolphin
leopard
whale
tiger

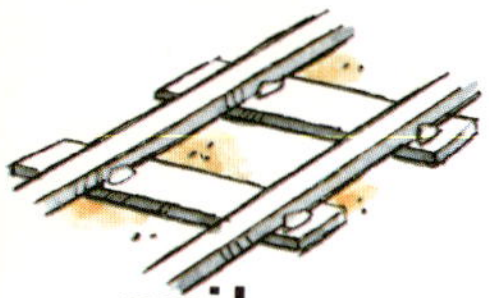
railway lines

guard

engine

buffers

buffet car

carriages

engine driver

goods train

platform

signals

ticket collector

The railway station

The garage

suitcases

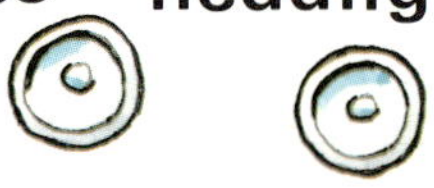
headlights

engine

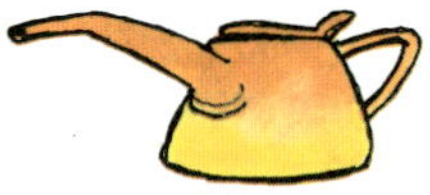
oil can

battery

petrol lorry

The airport

air hostess

helicopter

runway

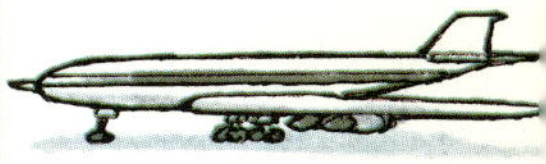
aeroplane

control tower

pilot

car wash

boot

air pump

wheel

spanner

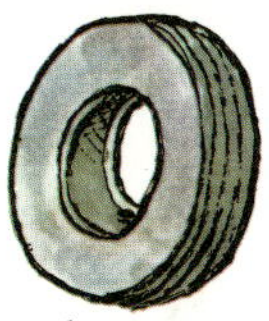
tyre

bonnet

breakdown lorry

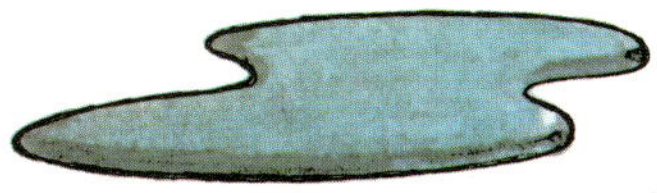
oil

petrol pump

The country

windmill

forest

hut

rabbits

moth

fox

stream

sign post

flowers

squirrel

butterfly

birds

badger

hill

fox cubs

tunnel

village

owl

balloon
caravan
logs
tents
road
bridge
barge
waterfall
mountain
stones
mole
ock
fisherman
rocks
canal
train
river

The farm

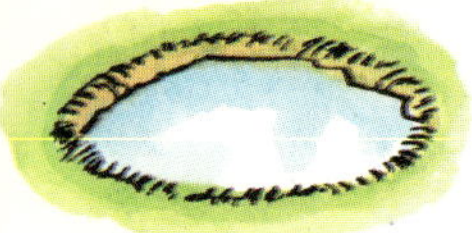
pond

sheep

haystack

ducks

trailer

lambs

fence

loft

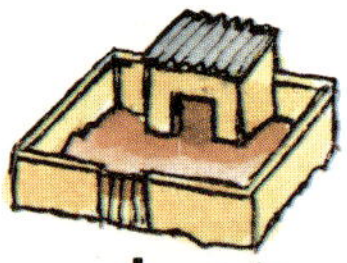
pigsty

bull

mud

piglets

barn

stable

cart

farmer

pony

tractor

saddle

geese

straw bales

sacks

lorry
orchard
hen house
cowshed
cow
ducklings
cock
calf
plough
shepherd
sheep dog
turkeys
scarecrow
farmhouse
corn
field
hay
goslings
horse
pigs
chicks
hens

The seaside

sailing boat

sea

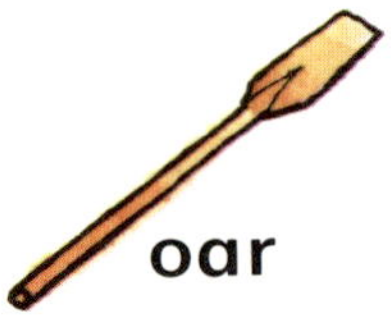
oar

lighthouse

spade

bucket

star fish

sandcastle

gull

flag

crab

sailor

sun hat

buoy

island

harbour

deck chair

motor boat

water skier

waves
seashell
cliff
ship
canoe
pebbles
ball
rocks
flippers
sea weed
net
paddle
fishing boat
mbrella
donkey
oil tanker
rowing boat
swimsuit
rope

At school

aquarium

badge

ceiling

pencils

boys

calendar

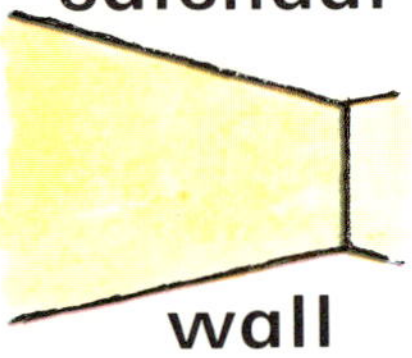

wall

wastepaper bin

scissors

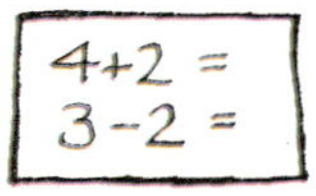

sums

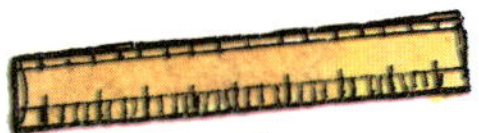

ruler

desk

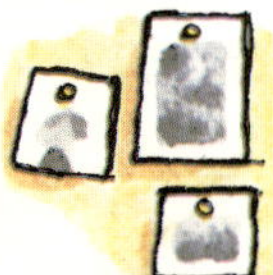

photographs

paints

paper

brushes

bell

a b c d e f g
h i j k l m n o
p q r s t u v
w x y z

alphabet

boxes

books

a b c d e f g
h i j k l m n o
p q r s t u v
painting
pens
chalk
easel
floor
plants
girls
globe
glue
door handle
note book
drawing pins
rawing
map
crayons
lamp
blackboard
blind
rubber
teacher

trolley

crutches

cotton wool

teddy bear

lift

glass

porter

dressing gown

pills

In hospital

nurse

tray

flowers

curtain

comic

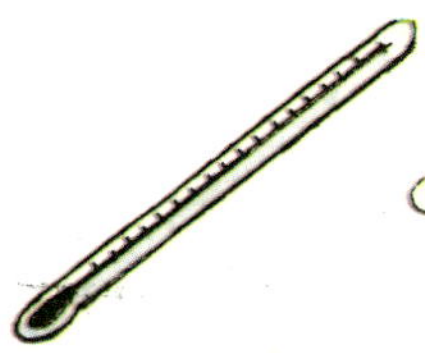
thermometer

doll

watc

locker

medicine

slippers

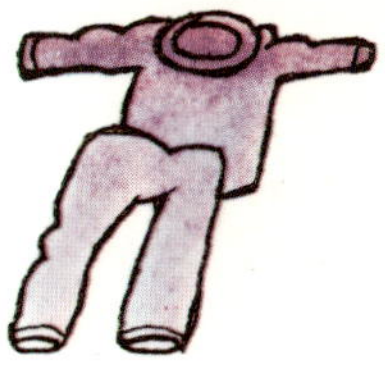

pyjamas

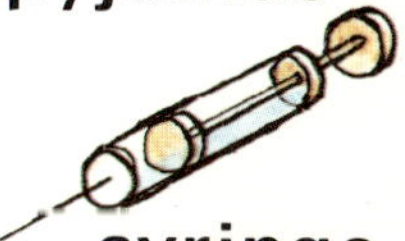

syringe

squash

nightdress

cupboard

television

bed

chart

plaster

bandage

black eye

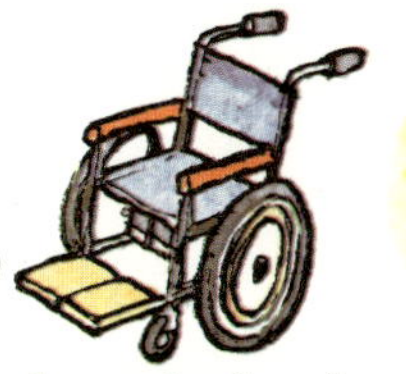

wheelchair

jigsaw

doctor

balloons

sparklers

paper hats

trifle

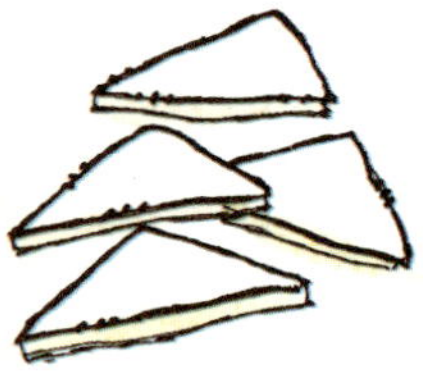
sandwiches

moon

sweets

biscuits

The party

table cloth

records

cake

chocolate

buns

lanter

toys

ribbon

candles

straws

stars

parcels

pudding

presents

window

jelly

fireworks

paper chains

costume

bananas

grapefruit

lettuce

grapes

cauliflower

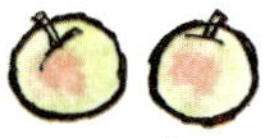
apples

carrots

leek

pumpkin

cucumber

lemons

celery

beans

cherries

apricots

cabbage

melon

The shop

mushrooms

tomatoes

peas

plums

raspberries

onions

peaches

pineapple

potatoes

spinach

FISH
BREAD
GROCERIES
tins
bread
butter
cheese
chicken
eggs
fish
flour
jars
meat
sausages
yoghurt
basket
bottles
routs
oranges
strawberries
bags
cash desk
scales
money
purse
trolley
handbag

Food

breakfast

lunch or dinner

coffee

chicken

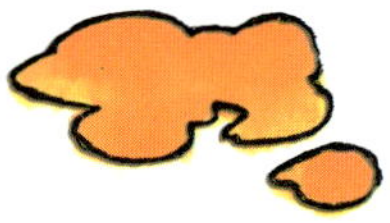

jam

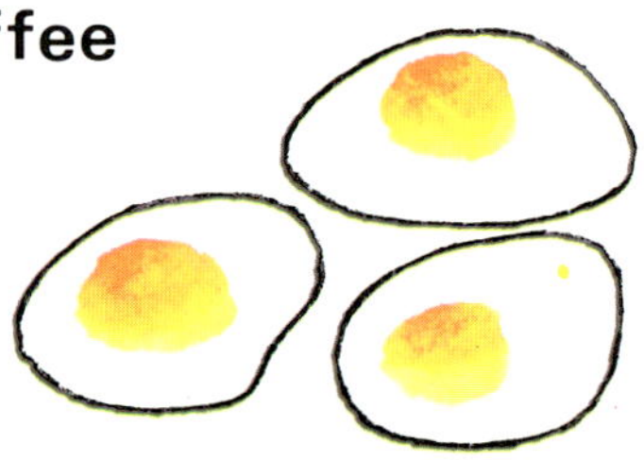

fried eggs

milk

honey

hot chocolate

chops

cream

beer

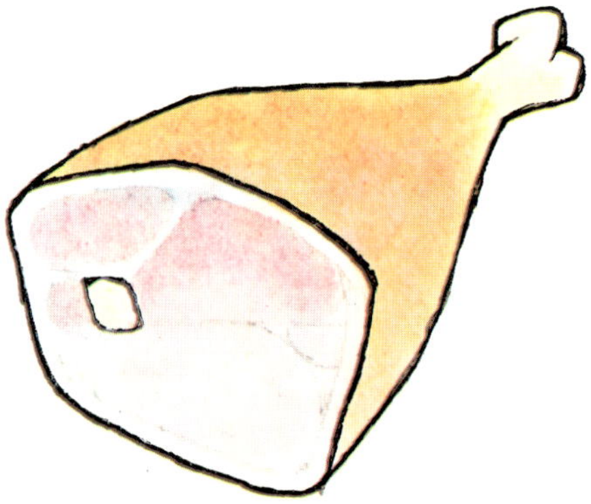

ham

salt

pepper

supper or dinner

tea

fruit juice

nuts

meat

omelette

salad

sugar

soup

rolls

pancakes

stew

rice

wine

spaghetti

sauce

Me

hair
eyebrow
eye
nose
cheek
mouth
lips
teeth
tongue
chin
neck
ears
head
face
shoulders
arms
elbow
hands
fingers
thumbs
back
bottom
chest
tummy
knees
legs
feet
toes
heel

My clothes

pants
vest
trousers
jeans
t-shirt
skirt
shirt
tie
shorts
socks
sweater
jumper
cardigan
tights
blouse
dress
gymshoes
shoes
sandals
boots
gloves
jacket
anorak
coat
handkerchief
cap
hat
belt
buttons
button holes
pockets
zip
buckle
laces
scarf

People

actor

chef

dancer

frogman

astronaut

conductor

carpenter

clown

shop-keeper

soldier

policeman

farmer

singer

racing-car driver

mechanic

artist

fireman
butcher
postman
deep-sea diver
painter
train driver
mountaineer
dentist
pilot
judge
zoo-keeper
baker

Families

father
husband
mother
wife
daughter
sister
son
brother
aunt
uncle
cousin
grandmother
grandfather

Doing things

low
climb
play
cook
fight
sleep
wait
skip
pick
watch
throw
talk
take
pull
eat
sew
jump
dig
sing
win
run
stand
make
buy
walk
push

Opposite words

slow
fast
easy
difficult
long
short
upstairs
downstairs
nice
nasty
over
under
front
back
wet
dry
alive
dead
dark
light
open
closed
right
old
new
out
in

Storybook words

devil
crown
palace
pageboy
princess
sword
queen
king
prince
angel
prison
dinosaur
wizard
reindeer
sleigh
Father Christmas
bridegroom
bridesmaids
bride
ghost
monster

Pets

rabbits
cat
dog
goldfish
lizards
parrot
frogs
hedgehog
budgerigars
silk worms
hamster
toads
pigeons
puppies
mice
snakes
kittens
tortoises

Weather

clouds

fog

rain

frost

snow

sun

rainbow

lightning

dew

wind

mist

Seasons

spring

summer

autumn

winter

Sports

boxing

cycle racing

baseball

swimming

football

gymnastics

high jump

skiing

motor racing

tennis

horse racing

skating

shooting

cricket

weight-lifting

show jumping

speedway racing

riding

sailing

table tennis

rowing

wrestling

basket ball

judo

Colours

Shapes

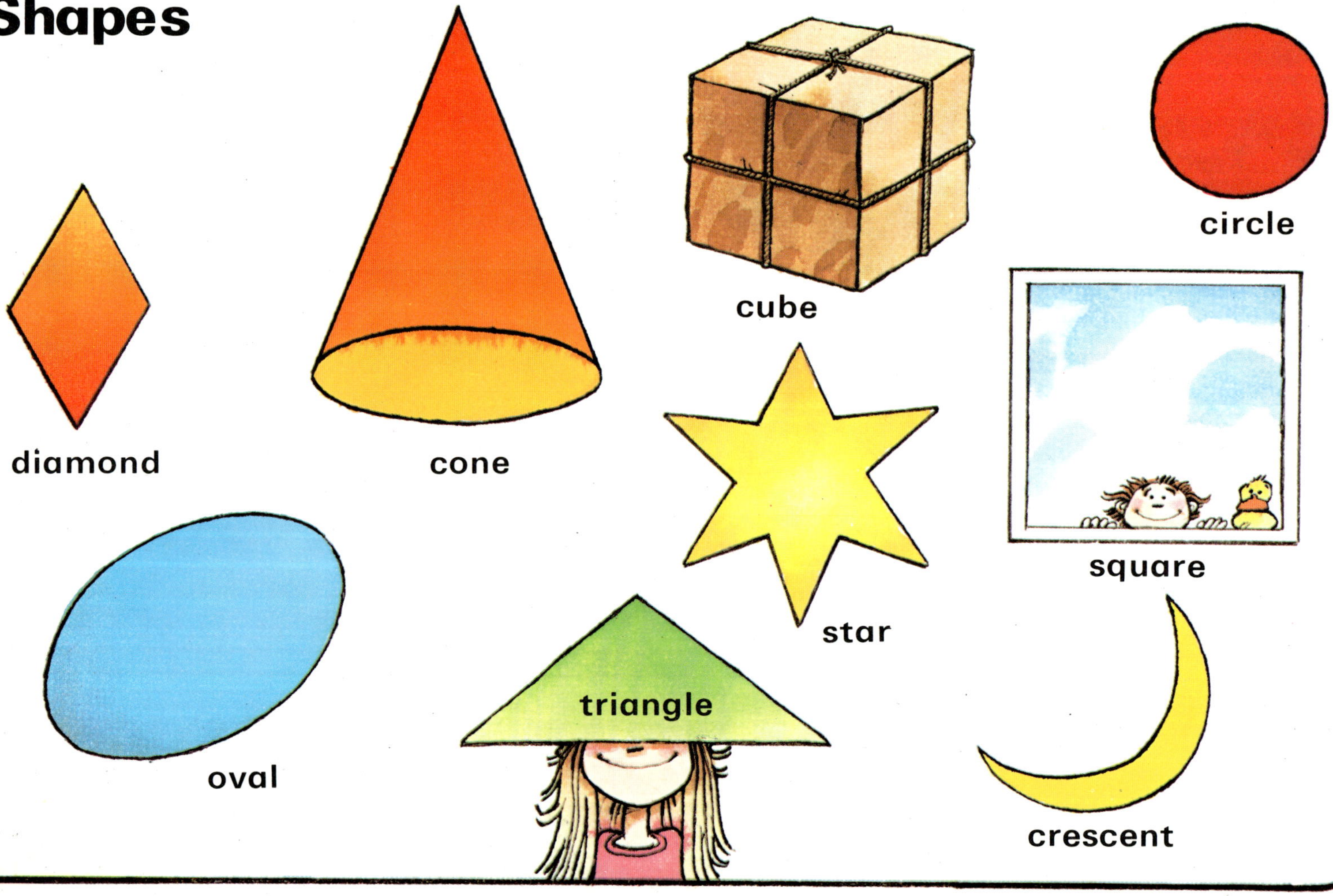

Numbers

1 one

2 two

3 three

4 four

5 five

6 six

7 seven

8 eight

9 nine

10 ten

11 eleven

12 twelve

13 thirteen

14 fourteen

15 fifteen

16 sixteen

17 seventeen

18 eighteen

19 nineteen

20 twenty

The fairground

roundabout

mat

helter skelter

big wheel

dodgems

big dipper

hoop-la

pop corn

candy floss

ghost train

rifle range

The circus

pole
trapeze
tight-rope walker
tight rope
band
safety net
rope ladder
juggler
acrobats
lion tamer
whip
lion
trick cyclist
bare-back rider
hoop
ring master
dog
clown

Auf den folgenden Seiten sind alle Wörter dieses Buches in alphabetischer Reihenfolge aufgeführt. Hinter jedem Wort steht die Seitenzahl, eine Aussprache-Hilfe und die deutsche Übersetzung.
Schüler, die mit einer Fremdsprache beginnen, werden die Lautschrift zunächst nicht verwenden, sondern die Aussprache mit dem Lehrer üben. Später wird die Lautschrift allerdings in den Lehrplan aufgenommen, damit der Sprachschüler den Umgang mit Wörterbüchern und der darin enthaltenen Lautschrift erlernt. Am besten ist es natürlich immer, die Aussprache mit einem Partner zu üben, der die Fremdsprache beherrscht.

Erklärung der Lautschrift

[ʌ]	kurzes *a*, etwa wie in dt. m*a*tt
[ɑ:]	langes *a*, etwa wie in dt. l*ah*m
[ai]	etwa wie in dt. *Ei*s, f*ei*n
[au]	etwa wie in dt. Fr*au*, H*au*s
[æ]	mehr zum *a* hin als dt. *ä* in W*ä*sche
[e]	kurzes *e*, wie in dt. B*e*tt
[ei]	nicht wie in dt. *Ei*, sondern *e-i*, d. h. von [e] zu [i] gleiten
[ɛə]	*ä* wie in dt. B*ä*r, dann zu [ə] gleiten
[ə]	kurzes, unbetontes *e*, etwa wie in dt. grüß*e*n, bitt*e*
[ə:]	etwa wie in dt. K*ö*rner (aber ohne *r*!)
[əu]	von [ə] zu [u] gleiten
[f]	stimmloser Lippenlaut wie im Deutschen *f*lott
[i]	kurzes *i*, etwa wie in dt. m*i*t
[i:]	langes *i*, etwa wie in dt. n*ie*, L*ie*be
[iə]	von kurzem [i] zu [ə] gleiten, kürzer als in dt. h*ier*
[j]	flüchtiger zwischen *j* und *i* schwebender Laut
[ɔ]	kurzes offenes *o*, etwa wie in dt. G*o*tt
[ɔ:]	langes offenes *o*, etwa wie in dt. K*o*rn (aber ohne *r*!)
[ɔi]	etwa wie in dt. n*eu*
[u]	kurzes *u*, etwa wie in dt. M*u*tter
[u:]	langes *u*, etwa wie in dt. Sch*uh*
[uə]	kürzer als in dt. K*ur*
[ŋ]	wie in dt. la*ng*e
[ŋk]	derselbe Laut mit nachfolgendem *k* wie im deutschen sen*k*en, Win*k*
[r]	nicht rollen! Zunge an den Gaumen und leicht zurückbiegen
[s]	wie in dt. rei*ß*en, wi*ss*en
[z]	wie in dt. rei*s*en, le*s*en
[θ]	wie *ß* in dt. Fa*ß*, aber gelispelt, d. h. Zunge an obere Vorderzähne
[ð]	wie *s* in dt. *s*att, aber gelispelt, d. h. Zunge an obere Vorderzähne
[ʃ]	wie in dt. Ti*sch*
[ʒ]	wie in dt. Gara*g*e, Lo*g*e
[v]	wie in dt. *W*ein, *V*ioline, *V*isum
[w]	nicht wie dt. *w*! Mit vorgestülpten Lippen bebildetes kurzes *u*, von dem man schnell zum nachfolgenden Laut übergleitet
[x]	stimmloser, hinten im Mund gebildeter Reibelaut wie *ch* in a*ch*
[:]	bedeutet, daß der vorangehende Laut lang gesprochen wird

Nützliche Wörter ohne Bilder

week	[wi:k]	Woche
Sunday	['sʌndi]	Sonntag
Monday	['mʌndi]	Montag
Tuesday	['tju:zdi]	Dienstag
Wednesday	['wenzdi]	Mittwoch
Thursday	['θə:zdi]	Donnerstag
Friday	['fraidi]	Freitag
Saturday	['sætədi]	Samstag

year	[jə:]	Jahr
January	['dʒænjuəri]	Januar
February	['februəri]	Februar
March	[ma:tʃ]	März
April	['eipril]	April
May	[mei]	Mai
June	[dʒu:n]	Juni
July	[dʒu(:)'lai]	Juli
August	['ɔ:gəst]	August
September	[səp'təmbə]	September
October	[ɔk'toubə]	Oktober
November	[no(u)'vembə]	November
December	[di'sembə]	Dezember

Merke: Bei vielen Wörtern gibt es mehrere Bedeutungen. Hier sind nur die den Bildern entsprechenden Begriffe angegeben.

acrobat, 55	['ækrəbæt]	der Akrobat
actor, 40	['æktə]	der Schauspieler
aerial, 13	['ɛəriəl]	die Fernsehantenne
air hostess, 21	[ɛə 'həustis]	die Stewardeß
airport, 21	[~pɔ:t]	der Flughafen
air pump, 21	[~ pʌmp]	die Luftpumpe
alive, 45	[ə'laiv]	lebendig
alphabet, 28	['ælfəbit]	das Alphabet
ambulance, 12	['æmbjuləns]	der Krankenwagen
ape, 19	[eip]	der Affe
apple, 34	['æpl]	der Apfel
apricot, 34	['eiprikɔt]	die Aprikose
apron, 6	['eiprən]	die Schürze
aquarium, 28	[ə'kwɛəriəm]	das Aquarium
arm, 38	[a:m]	der Arm
armchair, 5	['a:m'tʃɛə]	der Sessel
arrow, 15	['ærəu]	der Pfeil
artist, 40	['a:tist]	der Maler
astronaut, 40	['æstrəunɔ:t]	der Astronaut
aunt, 41	[a:nt]	die Tante
autumn, 49	['ɔ:təm]	der Herbst
axe, 11	[æks]	das Beil

baby, 17	['beibi]	das Baby
back, 45	[bæk]	hinten
back (of body), 38	[~]	der Rücken
bad, 44	[bæd]	böse
badge, 28	[bædʒ]	das Abzeichen
badger, 24	[bædʒə]	der Dachs
bag, 35	[bæg]	die Tragtasche
baker, 4	['beikə]	der Bäcker
ball, 16, 27	[bɔ:l]	der Ball
balloon, 23, 32	[bə'lu:n]	der Ballon
banana, 34	[bə'nɑ:nə]	die Banane
band, 55	[bænd]	die Kapelle
bandage, 31	['bændidʒ]	der Verband
bare-back rider, 55	[bɛə bæk raɪdə]	die Reiterin
barge, 23	[bɑ:dʒ]	der Kahn
barn, 24	[bɑ:n]	die Scheune
barrel, 11	['bærəl]	das Faß
baseball, 50	[beis bɔ:l]	das Baseballspiel
basket, 35	['bɑ:skit]	der Korb
basketball, 51	[~ bɔ:l]	das Basketballspiel
bat (animal), 18	[bæt]	die Fledermaus
bat (for hitting), 14	[~]	der Schläger
bath, 4	[bɑ:θ]	die Badewanne
bath, have a (to), 42	[~]	baden
bathroom, 4	[~rum]	das Badezimmer
battery, 20	[bætəri]	die Batterie
bead, 14	[bi:d]	die Perle
bean (french), 34	[bi:n]	die Bohne
bear, 18	[bɛə]	der Bär
beaver, 18	[,bi:və]	der Biber
bed, 5, 31	[bed]	das Bett
bedroom, 5	[~rum]	das Schlafzimmer
bee, 9	[bi:]	die Biene
beehive, 8	[~ haiv]	der Bienenstock
beer, 36	[biə]	das Bier
bell, 28	[bel]	die Glocke
belt, 39	[belt]	der Gürtel
bench (park), 17	[bentʃ]	die Bank
bench (work), 11	[~]	die Werkbank
bicycle, 12	['baisikl]	das Fahrrad
big, 44	[big]	groß
big dipper, 54	[~ 'dipə]	die Achterbahn
big wheel, 54	[~ wi:l]	das Riesenrad
bird, 17, 22	[bə:d]	der Vogel
birds'nest, 9	[~z' nest]	das Vogelnest
biscuit, 32	['biskit]	das Plätzchen
black, 52	[blæk]	schwarz
blackboard, 28	[~bɔ:d]	die Tafel
black eye, 31	[~ ai]	das blaue Auge
blind (window), 29	[blaind]	die Jalousie
block, 14	[blɔk]	der Baustein
blouse, 39	[blauz]	die Bluse
blow (to), 43	[bləu]	blasen
blue, 52	[blu:]	blau
boat, 15	[bəut]	das Boot
bolt, 9	[bəult]	der Bolzen
bone, 8	[bəun]	der Knochen
bonfire, 9	['bɔnfaiə]	das Feuer
bonnet (of car), 21	['bɔnit]	die Kühlerhaube
book, 28	[buk]	das Buch
bookcase, 4	[~ keis]	das Bücherregal
boot (for foot), 39	[bu:t]	der Stiefel
boot (for car), 21	[~]	der Kofferraum
bottle, 35	['bɔtl]	die Flasche
bottom (of body), 38	['bɔtəm]	der Popo
bottom (drawer), 44	[~]	die unterste
bow, 15	[bau]	der Bogen
bowl, 7	[bəul]	die Schüssel
box, 28	[bɔks]	die Schachtel
boxing, 50	[bɔksiŋ]	das Boxen
boy, 28	[bɔi]	der Junge
bread, 35	[bred]	das Brot
break (to), 42	[breik]	zerbrechen
breakdown lorry, 21	[breikdaun 'lɔri]	der Abschleppwagen
breakfast, 36	['brekfəst]	das Frühstück
brick, 8	[brik]	der Ziegelstein
bride, 47	[braid]	die Braut
bridegroom, 47	[~ grum]	der Bräutigam
bridesmaid, 47	[braidzmeid]	die Brautjungfer
bridge, 23	[bridʒ]	die Brücke
broom, 7, 9	[bru:m]	der Besen
broomstick, 46	['brumstik]	der Besenstiel
brother, 41	['brʌðə]	der Bruder
brown, 52	[braun]	braun
brush, 5, 7, 28	[brʌʃ]	der Pinsel, die Bürste
bubbl, 4	['bʌbl]	die Blase
bucket, 26	['bʌkit]	der Eimer
buckle, 39	['bʌkl]	die Schnalle
budgerigar, 48	[bʌdʒəriga:]	der Wellensittich
buffalo, 19	['bʌfələu]	der Büffel
buffer (train), 20	['bʌfə]	der Puffer
buffet car, 20	['bufei ka:]	der Speisewagen
build (to), 42	[bild]	bauen
bulb (light), 7	[bʌlb]	die Birne
bull, 24	[bul]	der Stier
bun, 32	[bʌn]	das Rosinenbrötchen
bun, 32	[bɔi]	die Boje
bus, 13	[bʌs]	der Bus
bush, 16	[buʃ]	der Busch
butcher, 41	['butʃə]	der Metzger
butter, 35	['bʌtə]	die Butter
butterfly, 22	[~ flai]	der Schmetterling
button, 39	['bʌtn]	der Knopf
button hole, 39	[~ həul]	das Knopfloch
buy (to), 43	[bai]	einkaufen

cabbage, 34	['kæbidʒ]	der Kohl
café, 12	['kæfei]	das Café
cake, 32	[keik]	der Kuchen
calendar, 28	['kælində]	der Kalender
calf, 25	[ka:f]	das Kalb
camel, 19	['kæməl]	das Kamel
camera, 14	['kæmərə]	der Fotoapparat
canal, 23	[kə'næl]	der Kanal
candle, 33	['kændl]	die Kerze
candy floss, 54	['kændi flɔs]	die Zuckerwatte
cannon, 14, 46	['kænən]	die Kanone
canoe, 27	[kə'nu']	das Kanu
cap, 39	[kæp]	die Mütze
car, 13	[ka:]	das Auto
cardigan, 39	['ka:digən]	die Strickjacke
carpenter, 40	['ka:pintə]	der Zimmermann
carpet, 4	['ka:pit]	der Teppich
carriage, 20	['kæridʒ]	der Waggon

carrot, 34	['kærət]	die Karotte
carry (to), 42	['kæri]	tragen
cart, 24	[kɑ:t]	der Karren
cash desk, 35	[kæʃ desk]	die Kasse
castle, 15, 46	['kɑ:sl]	die Burg
cat, 48	[kæt]	die Katze
catch (to), 42	[kætʃ]	fangen
caterpillar, 8	['keitə'pilə]	die Raupe
cauliflower, 34	['kɔliflauə]	der Blumenkohl
ceiling, 27	[si'lɪŋ]	die Decke
celery, 34	['seləri]	der Sellerie
chalk, 29	[tʃɔ:k]	die Kreide
chart, 31	[tʃɑ:t]	die Fieberkurve
cheek, 38	[tʃi:k]	die Backe
cheese, 34, 35	[tʃi:z]	der Käse
chef, 40	[ʃef]	der Koch
cherry, 34	['tʃeri]	die Kirsche
chest (body), 38	[tʃest]	die Brust
chest of drawers, 5	[~ ɔv drɔ:əz]	die Kommode
chick, 25	[tʃik]	das Küken
chicken, 35, 36	['tʃikin]	das Huhn
child, 16	['tʃaild]	das Kind
chimney, 12	['tʃimni]	der Schornstein
chin, 38	[tʃin]	das Kinn
chocolate, 32	['tʃɔkəlit]	die Schokolade
chop (wood) (to), 42	[tʃɔp]	hacken
chop (meat), 36	[~]	das Kotelett
church, 13	[tʃɔ:tʃ]	die Kirche
cinema, 13	['sinəmə]	das Kino
circle, 52	['sə:kl]	der Kreis
circus, 55	['sə:kəs]	der Zirkus
clay, 15	[klei]	der Ton
clean, 44	[kli:n]	sauber
clean (to), 42	[~]	waschen
cliff, 27	[klif]	die Klippe
climb (to), 43	[klaim]	klettern
clock, 4, 6	[klɔk]	die Uhr
closed, 45	[kləuzd]	zu, geschlossen
clothes, 5, 39	[kləuðz]	die Kleider
cloud, 49	[klaud]	die Wolke
clown, 40, 55	[klaun]	der Clown
coat, 39	[kəut]	der Mantel
cobweb, 3	['kɔbweb]	die Spinnwebe
cock, 25	[kɔk]	der Hahn
coffee, 36	['kɔfi]	der Kaffee
cold, 44	[kəuld]	kalt
colour, 52	['kʌlə]	die Farbe
comb, 5	[kəum]	der Kamm
comic, 30	['kɔmik]	das Heft
conductor, 40	[kən'dʌktə]	der Dirigent
cone, 52	[kəun]	der Kegel
control tower, 21	[kən'trəul 'tauə]	der Kontrollturm
cook (to), 43	[kuk]	kochen
cooker, 7	[~ə]	der Herd
corn, 25	[kɔ:n]	das Getreide
costume, 33	[kɔstju:m]	das Kostüm
cotton wool, 30	['kɔtn wul]	die Watte
country, 22	['kʌntri]	das Land
cousin, 41	['kʌzn]	der Cousin
cow, 25	[kau]	die Kuh
cowboy, 46	['kaubɔi]	der Cowboy
cowshed, 25	[kauʃed]	der Kuhstall
crab, 26	[kræb]	der Krebs
crane, 14	[krein]	der Kran
crawl (to), 42	[krɔ:l]	kriechen
crayon, 29	['kreiən]	der Buntstift
cream, 36	[kri:m]	die Sahne
crescent, 52	['kresnt]	die Sichel
cricket (sport), 51	['krikit]	das Kricket
crocodile, 18	['krɔkədail]	das Krokodil
crossing, 12	[krɔsiŋ]	der Zebrastreifen
crown, 46	[kraun]	die Krone
crutch, 30	[krʌtʃ]	die Krücke
cry (to), 42	[krai]	weinen
cube, 52	[kju:b]	der Würfel
cucumber, 34	['kju:kʌmbə]	die Gurke
cup, 7	[kʌp]	die Tasse
cupboard, 7, 31	['kʌbəd]	der Schrank

curtain, 30	['kə:tn]	der Vorhang
cushion, 4	['kuʃən]	das Kissen
cut (to), 42	[kʌt]	mähen
cycle racing, 50	['saikl 'reisiŋ]	das Radrennen

dance (to), 42	[dɑ:ns]	tanzen
dancer, 40	[~ə]	die Tänzerin
dark, 45	[dɑ:k]	dunkel
daughter, 41	['dɔ:tə]	die Tochter
dead, 45	[ded]	tot
deck chair, 26	[dek tʃɛə]	der Liegestuhl
deep-sea diver, 40	[di:p si: daivə]	der Tiefseetaucher
deer, 19	[diə]	der Hirsch
dentist, 41	[dentist]	der Zahnarzt
desert, 46	['dezət]	die Wüste
desk, 28	[desk]	das Pult
devil, 47	['devl]	der Teufel
dew, 49	[dju:]	der Tau
diamond, 52	['daiəmənd]	der Rhombus
dice, 14	[dais]	der Würfel
difficult, 45	['difikəlt]	schwierig
dig (to), 43	[dig]	graben
digger, 13	['digə]	Bagger
dinner, 36, 37	['dinə]	das Abendessen
dinosaur, 47	['dainəusɔ:]	der Dinosaurier
dirty, 44	[dɔ:ti]	schmutzig
doctor, 31	['dɔktə]	der Doktor
dodgems, 54	['dɔdʒəm]	der Autoscooter
dog, 16, 48, 55	[dɔg]	der Hund
dog lead, 17	[~ led]	die Hundeleine
doll, 14, 30	[dɔ]	die Puppe
dolls'house, 14	[~z'haus]	das Puppenhaus
dolphin, 19	['dɔlfin]	der Delphin
donkey, 27	['dɔŋki]	der Esel
door, 6	[dɔ']	die Tür
door handle, 28	[~ 'hændl]	die Türklinke
downstairs, 45	[daunstɛəz]	unten
dragon, 46	['drægən]	der Drache
drawer, 7	[drɔ:ə]	die Schublade
drawing, 29	['drɔ:iŋ]	die Zeichnung
drawing pin, 29	[~ pin]	die Reißzwecke
dress, 39	[dres]	das Kleid
dressing gown, 30	['dresiŋ gaun]	der Morgenrock
drill (road), 12	[dril]	der Preßlufthammer
drill (wood), 10	[~]	der Bohrer
drink (to), 42	[driŋk]	trinken
driver, 13	[draivə]	der Fahrer
drum, 15	[drʌm]	die Trommel
dry, 45	[drai]	trocken
duck, 17, 24	[dʌk]	die Ente
duckling, 17	['dʌkliŋ]	das Entchen
dustbin, 8	[dʌstbin]	der Mülleimer
duster, 6	[dʌstə]	das Staubtuch
dustpan, 7	[dʌstpæn]	die Schaufel
dwarf, 46	[dwɔ:f]	der Zwerg

eagle, 18	['i:gl]	der Adler
ear, 38	[iə]	das Ohr
earth, 17	[ə:θ]	die Erde
easel, 29	['i:zl]	die Staffelei
easy, 45	['i:zi]	einfach
eat (to), 43	[i:t]	essen
egg, 35	[eg]	das Ei
eiderdown, 5	['aidə daun]	die Dauendecke
eight, 53	[eit]	acht
eighteen, 53	['ei'ti:n]	achtzehn
elbow, 38	['elbəu]	der Ellbogen
elephant, 19	['elifənt]	der Elefant
eleven, 53	[i'levn]	elf
elf, 46	[elf]	die Elfe
empty, 44	['empti]	leer
engine (car), 20	['endʒin]	der Motor
engine (railway), 20	[~]	der Motor

engine driver, 20	[~ draɪvə]	der Lokomotivführer
eye, 38	[ai]	das Auge
eyebrow, 38	[aibrau]	die Augenbraue
face, 38	[feis]	das Gesicht
factory, 13	['fæktəri]	die Fabrik
fairground, 54	[fɛəgraund]	der Jahrmarkt
fairy, 46	['fɛəri]	die Fee
fall (to), 42	[fɔ:l]	fallen
family, 41	['fæmili]	die Familie
far, 44	[fɑ:]	weit
farm, 24	[fɑ:m]	der Bauernhof
farmer, 24, 40	[~ə]	der Bauer
farmhouse, 25	[~haus]	das Bauernhaus
fast, 45	[fɑ:st]	schnell
fat, 44	[fæt]	dick
father, 41	['fɑ:ðə]	der Vater
Father Christmas, 47	[~ 'krisməs]	der Weihnachtsmann
feather, 18	['feðə]	die Feder
fence, 24	[fens]	der Zaun
few, 44	[fju:]	wenige
field, 25	[fi:ld]	der Acker
fifteen, 53	['fif'ti:n]	fünfzehn
fight (to), 42	[fait]	raufen
file, 10	[fail]	die Feile
finger, 38	[fiŋgə]	der Finger
fire, 9	['faiə]	das Feuer
fire engine, 13	[~ 'endʒin]	die Feuerwehr
fireman, 41	[~mæn]	der Feuerwehrmann
firewood, 10	[~wud]	das Brennholz
firework, 33	[~wə:k]	das Feuerwerk
first, 44	[fə:st]	der erste
fish, 35	[fiʃ]	der Fisch
fisherman, 23	['fiʃəmən]	der Angler
fiohing boat, 27	['fiʃiŋ bəut]	dao Fioohorboot
fishing rod, 15	[fiʃiŋ rɔd]	die Angelrute
five, 53	[faiv]	fünf
flag, 26	[flæg]	die Fahne
flat, 12	[flæt]	die Wohnung
flipper, 27	['flipə]	die Flosse
floor, 29	[flɔ:]	der Boden
flour, 35	['flauə]	das Mehl
flower, 8, 17, 22, 30	[~]	die Blume
flowerbed, 17	[~bed]	das Blumenbeet
fly, 5	[flai]	die Fliege
fog, 49	[fɔg]	der Nebel
food, 36	[fu:d]	das Essen
foot, 38	[fut]	der Fuß
football, 50	[~bɔ:l]	das Fußballspielen
forest, 22	['fɔrist]	der Wald
fork (garden), 9	[fɔ:k]	die Heugabel
fork (table), 6	[~]	die Gabel
four, 53	[fɔ:]	vier
fourteen, 53	['fɔ:'ti:n]	vierzehn
fox, 22	[fɔks]	der Fuchs
fox cub, 22	[fɔks kʌb]	der Welpe
fried egg, 36	[fraid eg]	das Spiegelei
frog, 16, 48	[frɔg]	der Frosch
frogman, 40	[~mæn]	der Froschmann
front, 45	[frʌnt]	vorne
frost, 49	[frɔst]	der Frost
fruit, 34	[fru:t]	das Obst
fruit juice, 37	[~ dʒu:s]	der Fruchtsaft
frying pan, 7	[fraiŋ pæn]	die Bratpfanne
full, 44	[ful]	voll
garage, 12, 20	['ærɑ:dʒ]	die Tankstelle
garden, 8	['gɑ'dn]	der Garten
gate, 16	[geit]	das Tor
ghost, 47	[gəust]	der Geist
ghost train, 54	[~ trein]	die Geisterbahn
giant, 46	['dʒaiənt]	der Riese
giraffe, 18	[dʒi'rɑ:f]	die Giraffe
girl, 29	[gə:l]	das Mädchen
glass (drinking), 6, 30	[glɑ:s]	das Glas
globe, 29	['gləub]	der Globus

glove, 39	[glʌv]	der Handschuh
glue, 29	[glu:]	der Klebstoff
goat, 19	[gəut]	die Ziege
goldfish, 48	[gəuldfiʃ]	der Goldfisch
good, 44	[gud]	gut
goods train, 20	[gudz trein]	der Güterzug
goose, 24	[gu:s]	die Gans
gorilla, 18	[gə'rilə]	der Gorilla
gosling, 25	['gɔzliŋ]	das Gänschen
grandfather, 41	[grænd'fɑðə]	der Großvater
grandmother, 41	['grændmʌðə]	die Großmutter
grape, 33	[greip]	die Weintraube
grass, 9	[grɑ:s]	das Gras
green, 52	[gri:n]	grün
greenhouse, 9	[~haus]	das Gewächshaus
grey, 52	[grei]	grau
groceries, 35	['grəusəriz]	die Lebensmittel
guard (railway), 20	[gɑ:d]	der Schaffner
guitar, 14	[gi'tɑ:]	die Gitarre
gull, 26	[gʌl]	die Möwe
gun, 15	[gʌn]	das Gewehr
gutter, 8	['gʌtə]	die Dachrinne
gymnastic, 50	['dʒimnæstik]	das Turnen
gymshoe, 39	[dʒimʃu']	der Turnschuh
hair, 38	[hɛə]	das Haar
half, 44	[hɑ:f]	halb
hall, 5	[hɔ:l]	der Vorraum
ham, 36	[hæm]	der Schinken
hammer, 10	['hæmə]	der Hammer
hamster, 48	['hæmstə]	der Hamster
hand, 38	[hænd]	die Hand
handbag, 35	[~bæg]	die Handtasche
handkerchief, 39	['hæŋkətʃif]	das Taschentuch
handle (door), 29	[hændl]	die Türklinke
harbour, 26	['hɑ:bə]	der Hafen
hard, 44	[hɑ:d]	hart
hat, 39	[hæt]	der Hut
hay, 25	[hei]	das Heu
haystack, 24	[~stæk]	der Heuschober
head, 38	[hed]	der Kopf
headlight, 20	[~lait]	der Scheinwerfer
hedge, 8	[hedʒ]	die Hecke
hedgehog, 48	[~hɔg]	der Igel
heel, 38	[hi:l]	die Ferse
helicopter, 21	['helikɔptə]	der Hubschrauber
helter skelter, 54	['heltə'skeltə]	die Rutschbahn
hen, 25	[hen]	das Huhn
hen house, 25	[~ haus]	der Hühnerstall
hide (to), 42	[haid]	verstecken
high, 44	[hai]	hoch
high jump, 50	[~ dʒʌmp]	der Hochsprung
hill, 22	[hil]	der Hügel
hippopotamus, 18	[hipə'pɔtəməs]	das Nilpferd
hoe, 9	[həu]	die Hacke
hole, 12	[həul]	das Loch
home (at), 4	[həum]	zu Hause
hoop, 55	[hu:p]	der Reifen
hoop-la, 54	['hu:plɑ:]	das Ringwerfen
horns, 19	[hɔ:ns]	das Geweih
horse, 25	[hɔ:s]	das Pferd
horse racing, 50	[~ reɪsɪŋ]	das Pferderennen
hose pipe, 9	[həuz paip]	der Schlauch
hospital, 30	['hɔspitl]	das Krankenhaus
hot, 44	[hɔt]	heiß
hot chocolate, 36	[~ 'tʃɔkəlit]	der Kakao
hotel, 12	[həu'tel]	das Hotel
house, 13	[haus]	das Haus
husband, 41	['hʌzbənd]	der Ehemann
hut, 22	[hʌt]	die Hütte
ice cream, 16	[ais kri:m]	das Eis
in, 45	[in]	innen
Indian, 46	['indjən]	der Indianer
iron, 6	['aiən]	das Bügeleisen
ironing board, 7	[~ bɔ:d]	das Bügelbrett
island, 26	['ailənd]	die Insel

jacket, 39	['dʒækit]	die Jacke
jam, 36	[dʒæm]	die Marmelade
jar, 10, 35	[dʒɑ:]	das Gefäß
jeans, 39	[dʒi:n]	die Jeans
jelly, 33	['dʒeli]	die Götterspeise
jigsaw, 31	['dʒigsɔ:]	das Puzzle
judge, 41	[dʒʌdʒ]	der Richter
judo, 51	['dʒu:dəu]	das Judo
juggler, 55	['dʒʌglə]	der Jongleur
jump (to), 43	[dʒʌmp]	springen
jumper, 39	[~ə]	der Pullover

kangaroo, 18	[kæŋgə'ru:]	das Känguruh
kettle, 6	['ketl]	der Kessel
key, 7	[ki:]	der Schlüssel
king, 47	[kiŋ]	der König
kitchen, 6	['kitʃin]	die Küche
kite, 16	[kait]	der Drachen
kitten, 48	['kitn]	das Kätzchen
knee, 38	[ni:]	das Knie
knife, 6	[naif]	das Messer
knight, 46	[nait]	der Ritter
knit (to), 42	[nit]	stricken

lace (shoe), 39	[leis]	das Schnürband
ladder, 11	['lædə]	die Leiter
lake, 17	[leik]	der See
lamb, 24	[læm]	das Lamm
lamp, 4, 29	[læmp]	die Lampe
lamp post, 13	['læmppəust]	der Laternenpfahl
lantern, 32	['læntən]	der Lampion
last, 44	[lɑ:st]	der letzte
laugh (to), 42	[lɑ:f]	lachen
lawn mower, 9	[lɔ:n mauə]	der Rasenmäher
leaf, 9	[li:f]	das Blatt
leek, 34	[li:k]	der Lauch
left, 44	[left]	links
leg, 38	[leg]	das Bein
lemon, 34	['lemən]	die Zitrone
leopard, 19	['lepəd]	der Leopard
letter, 5	['letə]	der Brief
lettuce, 34	['letis]	der Salat
lift, 30	[lift]	der Lift
light, 45	[lait]	hell
lighthouse, 26	[~haus]	der Leuchtturm
lightning, 49	['laitniŋ]	der Blitz
lion, 18, 55	['laɪən]	der Löwe
lion tamer, 55	[~ teimə]	der Löwenbändiger
lip, 38	[lip]	die Lippe
listen (to), 42	['lisn]	zuhören
living room, 4	['liviŋ ru:m]	das Wohnzimmer
lizard, 48	['lizəd]	die Eidechse
lock (canal), 23	[lɔk]	die Schleuse
locker, 31	[~ə]	der Nachttisch
loft, 24	[lɔft]	der Speicher
log, 23	[lɔg]	der Baumstamm
long, 45	[lɔŋ]	lang
lorry, 12, 25	['lɔri]	der Lastwagen
low, 44	[ləu]	niedrig
lunch, 36	[lʌntʃ]	das Mittagessen

magician, 46	[mə'dʒiʃən]	der Zauberer
make (to), 43	[meik]	basteln
man, 12	[mæn]	der Mann
many, 44	['meni]	viele
map, 29	[mæp]	die Landkarte
marble, 14	['mɑ:bl]	die Murmel
market, 3	['mɑ:kit]	der Markt
mask, 15	[mɑ:sk]	die Maske
mat, 54	[mæt]	die Matte
match, 7	['mætʃ]	das Zündholz
meat, 35, 37	[mi:t]	das Fleisch
mechanic, 40	[mi'kænik]	der Mechaniker
medicine, 31	[medsin]	die Medizin
melon, 34	['melən]	die Melone
milk, 36	[milk]	die Milch
mirror, 5	['mirə]	der Spiegel
mist, 49	[mist]	der Nebel
mole, 23	[məul]	der Maulwurf
money, 35	['mʌni]	das Geld
money box	[~ bɔks]	die Sparbüchse
monkey, 18	['mʌŋki]	der Affe
monster, 47	['mɔnstə]	das Ungeheuer
moon, 32	[mu:n]	der Mond
mop, 6	[mɔp]	der Mop
moth, 22	[mɔθ]	die Motte
mother, 41	['mʌðə]	die Mutter
motor boat, 26	['məutə bəut]	das Motorboot
motor cycle, 13	[~ saikl]	das Motorrad
motor racing, 50	[~ reisiŋ]	das Autorennen
mountain, 23	['mauntin]	der Berg
mountaineer, 41	[~niə]	der Bergsteiger
mouth, 38	[mauθ]	der Mund
mouth organ, 14	[~ 'ɔ:gən]	die Mundharmonika
mud, 24	[mʌd]	der Schlamm
mushroom, 34	['mʌʃrum]	der Pilz

nail, 11	[neil]	der Nagel
nasty, 45	['nɑ:sti]	scheußlich
near, 44	[niə]	nahe
neck, 38	[nek]	der Hals
net, 27	[net]	das Netz
new, 45	[nju:]	neu
newspaper, 5	[nju:zpeipə]	die Zeitung
nice, 45	[nais]	gut
nigthdress, 31	[naitdres]	das Nachthemd
nine, 53	[nain]	neun
nineteen, 53	[~'ti:n]	neunzehn
nose, 38	[nəuz]	die Nase
notebook, 29	[nəutbuk]	der Notizblock
number, 53	['nʌmbə]	die Zahl
nurse, 30	[nə's]	die Krankenschwester
nut (for bolts), 11	[nʌt]	die Mutter
nut (to eat), 37	[~]	die Nuß

oar, 26	[ɔ:]	das Ruder
oil, 21	[ɔil]	das Öl
oil can, 20	[kæn]	die Ölkanne
oil tanker, 26	[~ tænkə]	der Öltanker
old, 45	[əuld]	alt
omelette, 37	['ɔmlit]	das Omlett
one, 53	[wʌn]	eins
onion, 34	['ʌnjən]	die Zwiebel
open, 45	['əupən]	offen
opposite word, 44	['ɔpəzit wə:d]	das Gegenteil
orange (colour), 52	['ɔrindʒ]	orange
orange (fruit), 35	[~]	die Orange
orchard, 25	['ɔ:tʃəd]	der Obstgarten
ostrich, 18	['ɔstritʃ]	der Strauß
out, 45	[aut]	außen
oval, 52	['əuvəl]	das Oval
over, 45	['əuvə]	auf
owl, 22	[aul]	die Eule

paddle, 27	['pædl]	das Paddel
pageboy, 47	[peidʒbɔi]	der Page
paint (to), 42	[peint]	malen
paintbox, 15	[~boks]	der Malkasten
painter, 41	['peintə]	der Anstreicher
paint-pot, 10	[peintpot]	der Farbtopf
painting, 29	['peintiŋ]	das Bild
paint, 28	[peint]	die Farbe
palace, 47	['pælis]	der Palast
pancake, 37	['pænkeik]	der Pfannkuchen
panda, 18	[pændə]	der Pandabär
pants, 38	[pænts]	die Unterhose
paper, 28	[peipə]	das Papier

paper chain, 33	[~ tʃein]	die Girlande
paper hat, 32	[~ hæt]	der Hut
parachute, 15	['pærəʃu:t]	der Fallschirm
parcel, 33	['pɑ:sl]	das Paket
park, 16	[pɑ:k]	der Park
parrot, 48	['pærət]	der Papagei
party, 32	['pɑ:ti]	die Party
path, 9, 16	[pɑ:θ]	der Weg
pavement, 12	[peivment]	der Bürgersteig
paw, 18	[pɔ:]	die Klaue
pea, 34	[pi:]	die Erbse
peach, 34	[pi:tʃ]	der Pfirsich
pebble, 27	['pebl]	der Kiesel
peg (coat), 5	[peg]	der Haken
pelican, 18	['pelikən]	der Pelikan
pen, 29	[pen]	die Feder
pencil, 28	['pensl]	der Bleistift
penguin	['peŋgwin]	der Pinguin
penknife, 10	['pennaif]	das Taschenmesser
people, 40	['pi:pl]	die Leute
pepper, 36	['pepə]	der Pfeffer
pet, 48	[pet]	das Haustier
petrol lorry, 20	['petrəl 'lɔri]	der Tankwagen
petrol pump, 21	[~ pʌmp]	die Benzinzapfsäule
photograph, 28	['fəutəgra:f]	die Fotografie
piano, 14	['pjænəu]	das Klavier
pick (to), 43	[pik]	pflücken
picnic, 16	['piknik]	das Picknick
picture, 5	['piktʃə]	das Bild
pig, 25	[pig]	das Schwein
pigeon, 8, 48	['pidʒin]	die Taube
piglet, 24	[piglit]	das Ferkel
pigsty, 24	[pigstai]	der Schweinestall
pill, 36	[pil]	die Tablette
pillow, 5	['piləu]	das Kopfkissen
pilot, 21, 41	['pailət]	der Pilot
pineapple, 34	[painæpl]	die Ananas
pink, 52	[piŋk]	rosa
pipe, 13	[paip]	die Röhre
pirate, 46	[paiərit]	der Pirat
pistol, 46	['pistl]	die Pistole
plane (air), 21	[plein]	das Flugzeug
plane (wood), 11	[~]	der Hobel
plank, 10	[plænk]	das Brett
plant, 9, 29	[plɑ:nt]	die Pflanze
plaster, 31	['plɑ:stə]	der Gips
plate, 7	[pleit]	der Teller
platform, 20	['plætfɔ:m]	der Bahnsteig
play (to), 43	[plei]	spielen
playground, 12	[~graund]	der Spielplatz
playing card, 14	[~iŋ kɑ:d]	die Spielkarte
plough, 25	[plau]	der Pflug
plum, 34	[plʌm]	die Pflaume
pocket, 39	['pɔkit]	die Tasche
polar bear, 19	['pəulə bɛə]	der Eisbär
pole, 55	[pəul]	der Stab
police car, 12	[pə'li:s kɑ:]	die Funkstreife
policeman, 13, 40	[~mæn]	der Polizist
polish, 6	['pɔliʃ]	das Poliermittel
pond, 24	[pɔnd]	der Teich
pony, 24	['pəuni]	das Pony
popcorn, 54	['pɔpkɔ:n]	das Popcorn
porter, 30	['pɔ:tə]	der Pförtner
postman, 41	[pəustmæn]	der Postbote
pot (paint), 18	[pɔt]	der Farbtopf
potato, 34	[pə'teitəu]	die Kartoffel
pram, 9	[præm]	der Kinderwagen
present, 33	['preznt]	das Geschenk
prince, 47	[prins]	der Prinz
princess, 47	[prin'ses]	die Prinzessin
prison, 47	['prizn]	das Gefängnis
pudding, 33	['pudiŋ]	der Pudding
puddle, 17	[bnɪ]	die Pfütze
pull (to), 43	[,bvqɪ]	ziehen
pumpkin, 34	['pʌmpkin]	der Kürbis
puppet, 15	['pʌpit]	die Marionette
puppy, 48	['pʌpi]	das Hündchen
purple, 52	['pə:pl]	lila
push (to), 43	[puʃ]	schieben
push chair, 17	[~ tʃɛə]	der Kindersportwagen
pyjamas, 31	[pə'dʒɑ:məz]	der Schlafanzug
queen, 47	[kwi:n]	die Königin
rabbit, 21, 48	['ræbit]	das Kaninchen
racing car, 14	[reisiŋ kɑ:]	der Rennwagen
racing car driver, 40	[~ ~ draivə]	der Rennfahrer
radiator, 4	['reidieitə]	der Heizkörper
radio, 4	['reidiəu]	das Radio
railings, 17	['reiliŋs]	der Zaun
railway line, 20	['reilwei lain]	die Schiene
railway station, 20	[~ 'steiʃən]	der Bahnhof
rain, 49	[rein]	der Regen
rainbow, 49	[~bəu]	der Regenbogen
rake, 9	[reik]	der Rechen
raspberry, 30	['rɑ:zbəri]	die Himbeere
read (to), 42	[ri:d]	lesen
record, 32	['rekɔ:d]	die Schallplatte
recorder, 14	[ri'kɔ:də]	die Flöte
record player, 4	['rikɔ:d pleiə]	der Plattenspieler
red, 52	[red]	rot
refrigerator, 6	[ri'fridʒəreitə]	der Eisschrank
reindeer, 47	['reindiə]	das Rentier
rhinoceros, 19	[rai'nɔsərəs]	das Nashorn
ribbon, 33	['ribən]	das Band
rice, 37	[rais]	der Reis
riding, 51	[raidiŋ]	das Reiten
rifle range, 54	['raifl reindʒ]	die Schießbude
right, 45	[rait]	rechts
ring master, 55	[riŋ 'mɑ:stə]	der Zirkusdirektor
river, 23	['rivə]	der Fluß
road, 23	[rəud]	die Straße
robber, 46	[rɔbə]	der Räuber
robot, 14	['rəubɔt]	der Roboter
rocket, 15	['rɔkit]	die Rakete
rocking horse, 14	['rɔkiŋ hɔ's]	das Schaukelpferd
rock, 23, 27	[rɔk]	der Fels
roll (bread), 37	[rəul]	das Brötchen
roller, 12, 14	[~ə]	die Walze
roller skate, 16	[~ə skeit]	der Rollschuh
roof, 13	[ru:f]	das Dach
rope, 27	[rəup]	die Schnur
rope ladder, 55	[~ 'lædə]	die Strickleiter
roundabout, 54	['raundəbaut]	das Karussell
rowing, 51	[rəuiŋ]	das Rudern
rowing boat, 27	['rəuiŋbəut]	das Ruderboot
rubber, 28	['rʌbə]	der Radiergummi
rubbish, 7	['rʌbiʃ]	der Abfall
rug, 4	[rʌg]	der Vorleger
ruler, 28	[ru:lə]	das Lineal
run (to), 43	[rʌn]	laufen
runway, 21	['rʌnwei]	die Landebahn
sack, 24	[sæk]	der Sack
saddle, 24	['sædl]	der Sattel
safety net, 54	['seifti net]	das Sicherheitsnetz
sailing, 51	[seiliŋ]	das Segeln
sailing boat, 26	[~ bəut]	das Segelboot
sailor, 26	[seilə]	der Seemann
salad, 37	['sæləd]	der Salat
salt, 36	[sɔ:lt]	das Salz
sandal, 39	['sændl]	die Sandale
sandcastle, 26	[sændka:sl]	die Sandburg
sandpaper, 10	[~'peipə]	das Sandpapier
sandpit, 16	[~pit]	der Sandkasten
sandwich, 32	['sændwidʃ]	das belegte Brot
sauce, 37	[sɔ:s]	die Soße
saucepan, 6	[~pæn]	der Topf
saucer, 6	[~ə]	die Untertasse

sausage, 35	['sɔsidʒ]	die Wurst
saw (to), 10	[sɔ:]	die Säge
sawdust, 10	[~dʌst]	das Sägemehl
scale, 35	[skeil]	die Schuppe
scarecrow, 25	[skεəkrou]	die Vogelscheuche
scarf, 39	[skɑ:f]	der Schal
school, 12, 28	[sku:l]	die Schule
scissors, 28	['sizəz]	die Schere
scooter, 16	[sku:tə]	der Roller
screw, 11	[skru:]	die Schraube
screwdriver, 10	[~draivə]	der Schraubenzieher
sea, 26	[si:]	das Meer
sea shell, 27	[~ ʃel]	die Muschel
seal, 19	[si:l]	der Seehund
seaside, 26	[~said]	der Strand
season, 49	['si'zn]	die Jahreszeit
seaweed, 27	[si:wi:d]	die Alge
seed, 8	[si:d]	der Samen
seesaw, 17	['si:sɔ:]	die Wippe
seven, 53	['sevn]	sieben
seventeen, 53	[~ti:n]	siebzehn
sew (to), 43	[səu]	nähen
shape, 52	[ʃeip]	die Form
shark, 19	[ʃɑ:k]	der Haifisch
shavings, 16	['ʃeiviŋz]	die Späne
shed, 8	[ʃed]	der Schuppen
sheep, 24	[ʃi:p]	das Schaf
sheepdog, 25	[~dɔg]	der Schäferhund
sheet, 5	[ʃi:t]	das Bettlaken
shepherd, 25	['ʃepəd]	der Schäfer
sheriff, 46	['ʃerif]	der Sheriff
ship, 27	[ʃip]	das Schiff
shirt, 39	[ʃə:t]	das Hemd
shoe, 39	[ʃu:]	der Schuh
shooting, 51	['ʃu:tiŋ]	das Wettschießen
shop, 12, 34	[ʃɔp]	das Geschäft
shopkeeper, 40	[ʃɔpki:pə]	der Ladenbesitzer
short, 45	[ʃɔ:t]	kurz
shorts, 39	[ʃɔ:ts]	die kurze Hose
shoulder, 38	['ʃəuldə]	die Schulter
show jumping, 51	[ʃəu dʒʌmpiŋ]	der Hochsprung
shower, 4	['ʃauə]	die Brause
signal, 20	['signl]	das Signal
signpost, 22	[sainpoust]	der Wegweiser
silkworm, 48	[silkwə:m]	die Seidenraupe
sing (to), 43	[siŋ]	singen
singer, 40	['siŋə]	die Sängerin
sink, 6	[siŋk]	der Ausguß
sister, 41	['sistə]	die Schwester
sit (to), 42	[sit]	sitzen
six, 53	[siks]	sechs
sixteen, 53	[~'ti:n]	sechzehn
skating, 56	[skeitiŋ]	der Eislauf
skiing, 56	['ski:iŋ]	das Skilaufen
skip (to), 43	[skip]	hüpfen
skipping rope, 17	['skipiŋrəup]	das Springseil
skirt, 39	[skə:t]	der Rock
sleep (to), 43	[sli:p]	schlafen
sleigh, 47	[slei]	der Schlitten
slide, 16	[slaid]	die Rutschbahn
slipper, 31	[slipə]	der Pantoffel
slow, 45	[sləu]	langsam
small, 44	[smɔ:l]	klein
smile, 42	[smail]	lächeln
smoke, 9	[sməuk]	der Rauch
snail, 8	[sneil]	die Schnecke
snake, 48	[sneik]	die Schlange
snow, 49	[snəu]	der Schnee
soap, 4	[səup]	die Seife
sock, 39	[sɔk]	die Socke
soft, 44	[sɔft]	weich
soldier, 40	['səuldʒə]	der Soldat
soldier (toy), 15	[~]	der Bleisoldat
son, 41	[sʌn]	der Sohn
soup, 37	[su:p]	die Suppe
spaceman, 14	[speismæn]	der Astronaut
spade, 8, 26	[speid]	der Spaten
spaghetti, 37	[spə'geti]	die Spaghetti
spanner, 21	['spænə]	der Schraubenschlüssel
sparkle, 32	['spɑ:kl]	die Wunderkerze
speedway racing, 51	[spi:dwei reisiŋ]	das Motorradrennen
spider, 5	['spaidə]	die Spinne
spinach, 34	['spinidʒ]	der Spinat
sponge, 4	[spʌndʒ]	der Schwamm
spoon, 6	[spu:n]	der Löffel
sport, 50	[spɔ:t]	der Sport
spring, 49	[spriŋ]	der Frühling
sprinkler, 8	['spriŋklə]	der Rasensprenger
sprout, 35	[spraut]	der Rosenkohl
square, 52	[skwεə]	das Quadrat
squash, 31	[skwɔʃ]	der Obstsaft
squirrel, 22	['skwirəl]	das Eichhörnchen
stable, 24	['steibl]	der Stall
stagecoach, 46	[steidʒkoutʃ]	die Kutsche
stairs, 5	[stεəz]	die Stufe
stand (to), 43	[stænd]	stehen
star, 33, 52	[stɑ:]	der Stern
star fish, 26	['stɑ:fiʃ]	der Seestern
station, 20	['steiʃən]	der Bahnhof
statue, 13	['stættʃu:]	die Statue
step, 12	[step]	die Stufe
stew, 37	[stju:]	der Eintopf
stick, 9	[stik]	der Stock
stone, 23	[stəun]	der Stein
stool, 6	[stu:l]	der Hocker
story-book words, 46	['stɔ:ribuk]	Wörter in Märchen u. Gesch
straw (drinking), 33	[strɔ:]	der Strohhalm
straw bale, 24	[~ beil]	der Strohballen
strawberry, 35	[strɔ:bəri]	die Erdbeere
stream, 22	[stri:m]	der Bach
street, 12	[stri:t]	die Straße
string, 16	[striŋ]	die Schnur
submarine, 15	[sʌbmə'ri:n]	das U-Boot
sugar, 37	['ʃugə]	der Zucker
suitcase, 20	[swi:tkeis]	der Koffer
summer, 49	['sʌmə]	der Sommer
sums, 28	[sʌmz]	das Rechnen
sun, 49	[sʌn]	die Sonne
sun hat, 26	[~ hæt]	der Sonnenhut
supper, 37	['sʌpə]	das Abendessen
swan, 17	[swɔn]	der Schwan
sweater, 39	[swetə]	der Rollkragen
sweep (to), 42	[swi:p]	auffegen
sweet, 32	[swi:t]	das Bonbon
swimming, 50	['swimiŋ]	das Schwimmen
swimsuit, 27	[swimsju:t]	der Badeanzug
swing, 16	[swiŋ]	die Schaukel
switch, 6	[switʃ]	die Steckdose
sword, 47	[sɔ:d]	das Schwert
syringe, 31	['sirindʒ]	die Spritze

table, 4,7	['teibl]	der Tisch
table cloth, 32	[~ klɔ(:)θ]	die Tischdecke
table tennis, 51	[~ 'tenis]	das Tischtennis
tack, 10	[tæk]	der Reißnagel
tadpole, 16	['tædpəul]	die Kaulquappe
tail, 19	[teil]	die Schwanzflosse
take (to), 43	[teik]	nehmen
talk (to), 43	[tɔ:k]	erzählen
tank, 15	[tæŋk]	der Panzer
tap, 4	[tæp]	der Wasserhahn
tape measure, 11	[teip 'meʒə]	das Maßband
target, 15	['tɑ:git]	die Zielscheibe
taxi, 13	['tæksi]	das Taxi
tea, 37	[ti:]	der Tee
teacher, 29	[ti:tʃə]	die Lehrerin
teaspoon, 7	[ti:spu:n]	der Teelöffel
teddy bear, 30	['ted(i) bεə]	der Teddybär
telephone, 5	['telifəun]	das Telefon
televison, 31	['teliviʒən]	der Fernseher
ten, 53	[ten]	zehn
tennis, 50	[tenis]	das Tennis